Rhyme Time

PEARSON
Scott Foresman

Editorial Offices: Glenview, Illinois • Parsippany, New Jersey • New York, New York

Sales Offices: Needham, Massachusetts • Duluth, Georgia • Glenview, Illinois • Coppell, Texas • Sacramento, California • Mesa, Arizona

ISBN: 0-328-16888-2   Copyright © Pearson Education, Inc.

Illustrations   Cover: Holly Hannon; 1, 2, 4, 11, 22, 30, 32 Holly Hannon; 4, 6, 27 Jason Wolff; 4, 19, 21, 31 Jackie Snider: 7, 12 Ana Ochoa; 8, 13, 16 Nicole Inden-Bosch; 9, 17 Shelly Hehenberger; 10, 26 Chris Lensch; 14, 29 Chris Butler; 15 Eva Cockrille; 18 Terri Chickos; 20 Rose Mary Berlin; 23 Peter Lacalamita; 24 Brian Fujimori; 25 Daniel Mahoney; 28 Marion Eldridge

2 3 4 5 6 7 8 9 10 VO08 12 11 10 09 08 07 06 05

Contents

From A to Z

Hop on the bus,
Ride with me.

A B C D E F G

We'll ride along
From A to Z.

H I J K L M N O P

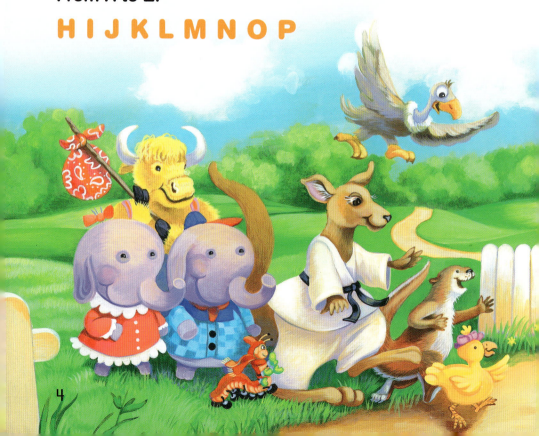

There are rhymes
For you and me.

Q R S T U V

This will be fun,
You will see.

W X Y and **Z**

Pick a letter, read a rhyme.
It is Ⓐ Ⓑ Ⓒ **Rhyme Time.**

The Ant and the Antelope

One afternoon an antelope
Jumps over a tiny ant.
The ant tries to jump over the antelope.
Do you think he can or can't?

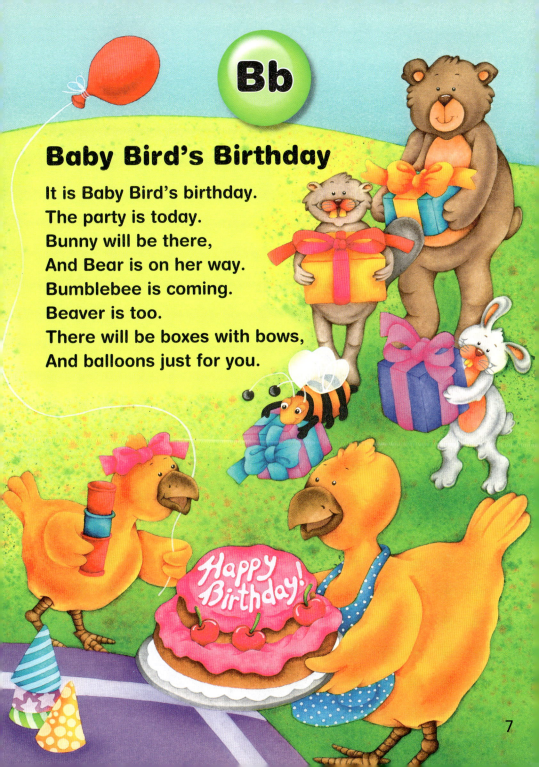

Bb

Baby Bird's Birthday

It is Baby Bird's birthday.
The party is today.
Bunny will be there,
And Bear is on her way.
Bumblebee is coming.
Beaver is too.
There will be boxes with bows,
And balloons just for you.

7

Cc

Cat in the Cupboard

Be careful!
Cat is in the cupboard.
Can you see her colorful eyes?
She might sneak around the corner
And catch us by surprise.

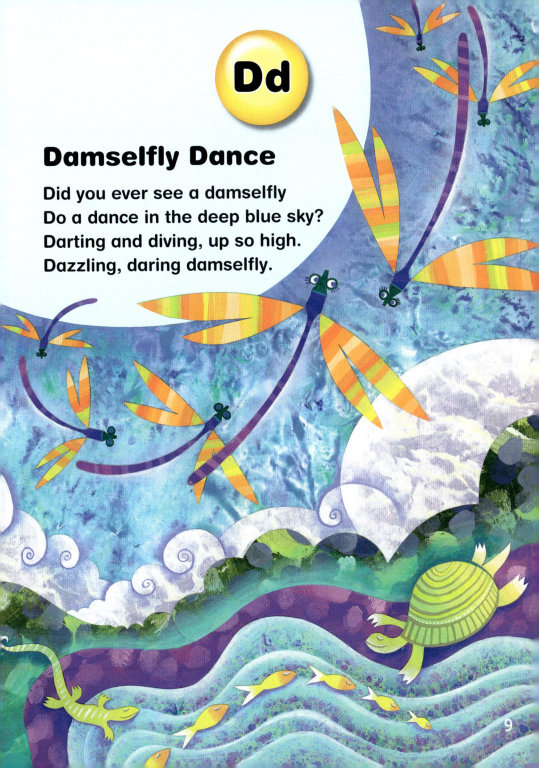

Dd

Damselfly Dance

Did you ever see a damselfly
Do a dance in the deep blue sky?
Darting and diving, up so high.
Dazzling, daring damselfly.

Enter and Exit

Elephants enter an empty elevator
To enjoy rides to higher floors,
They don't ever forget to exit
When the elevator opens its doors!

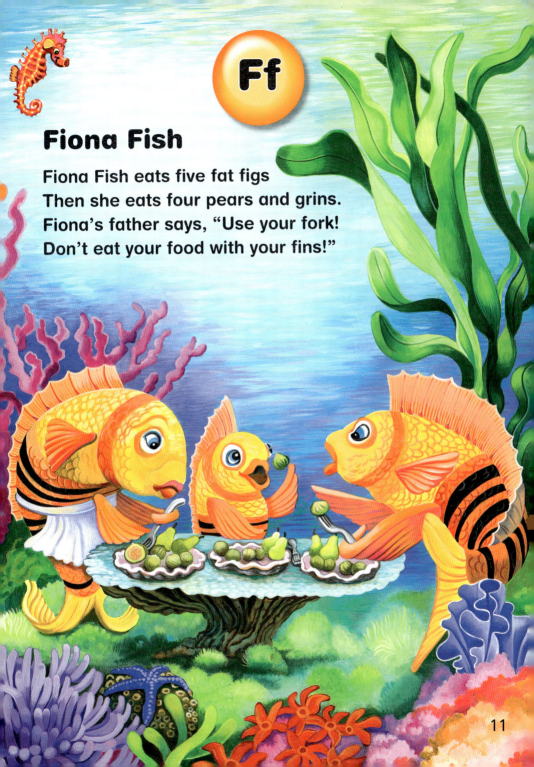

Ff

Fiona Fish

Fiona Fish eats five fat figs
Then she eats four pears and grins.
Fiona's father says, "Use your fork!
Don't eat your food with your fins!"

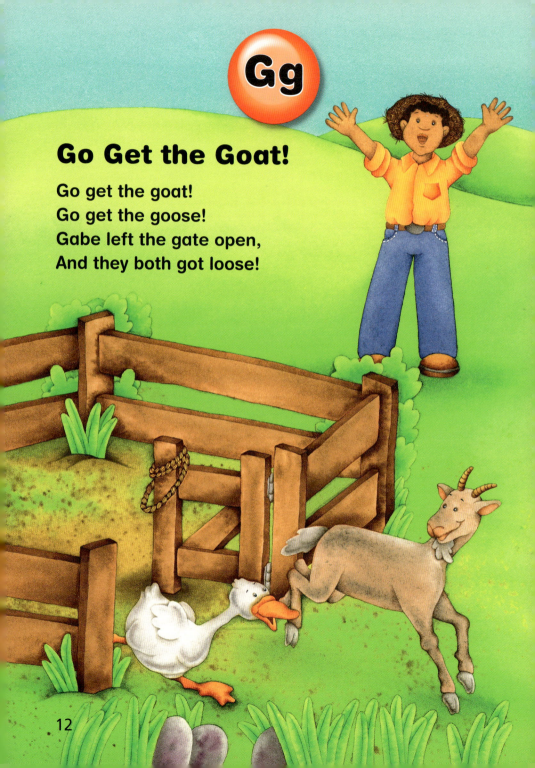

Gg

Go Get the Goat!

Go get the goat!
Go get the goose!
Gabe left the gate open,
And they both got loose!

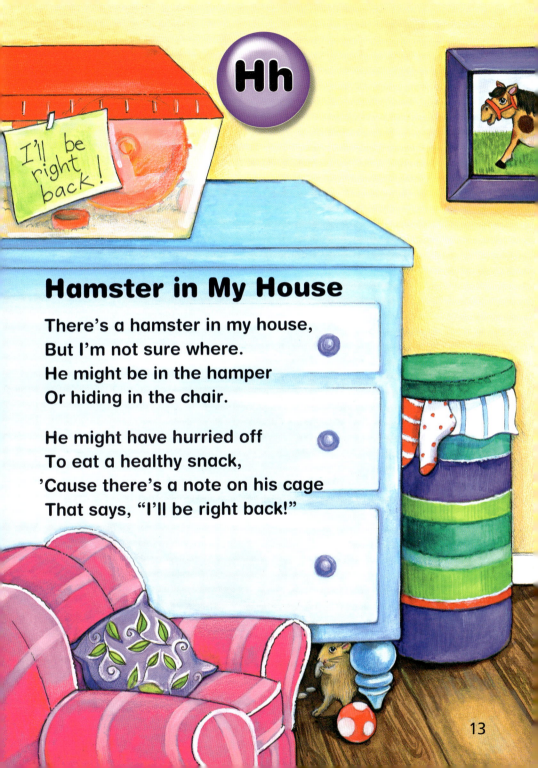

Hamster in My House

There's a hamster in my house,
But I'm not sure where.
He might be in the hamper
Or hiding in the chair.

He might have hurried off
To eat a healthy snack,
'Cause there's a note on his cage
That says, "I'll be right back!"

13

Iggy Inchworm

Iggy Inchworm inched along
An igloo, inch by inch.
If Iggy were a bit bigger,
This trip would be a cinch!

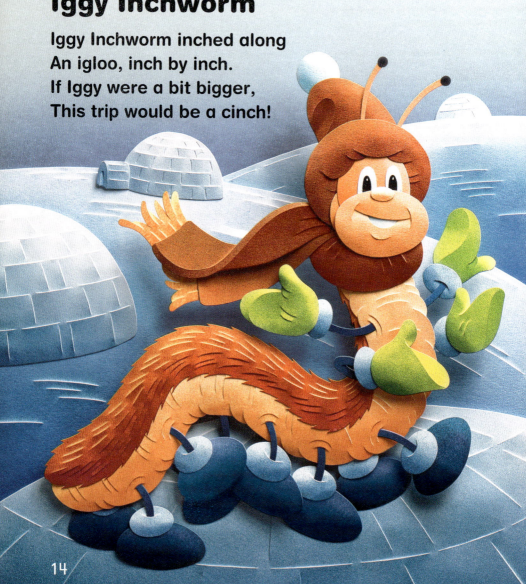

Joyful Jackrabbit

Joyful little jackrabbit,
Jogging through the town.
You're such a jolly joker,
Jumping up and down.

Are you wearing jammies
Or just a furry jacket?
Goodness, little jackrabbit,
You're making such a racket!

Karate Kangaroo

A kid from Kansas
Rode his bike to the zoo
And did karate kicks
With a kind kangaroo.

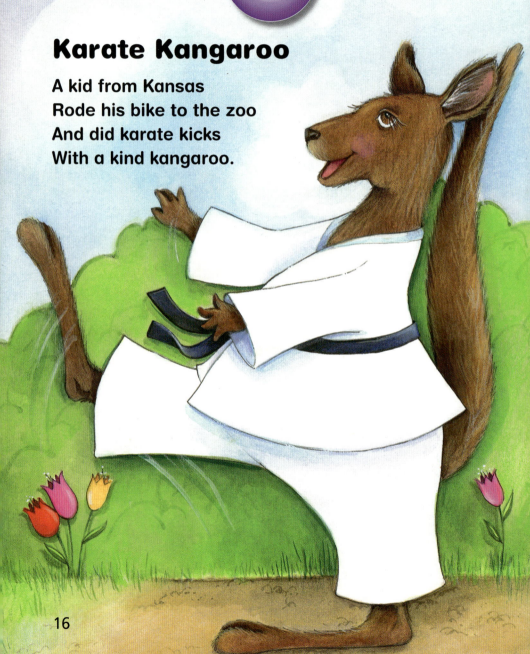

16

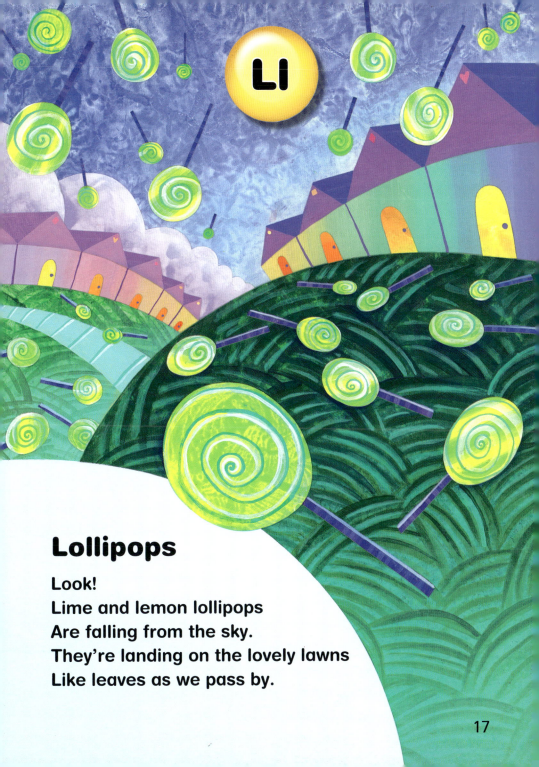

Lollipops

Look!
Lime and lemon lollipops
Are falling from the sky.
They're landing on the lovely lawns
Like leaves as we pass by.

17

Mister Monkey's Muffins

Mister Monkey munched on muffins
In the middle of my tree.
He made so many for himself,
But he didn't make any for me.

Neighbor Newt

My next-door neighbor is a little newt.
He wears a necktie and a suit.
He nibbles nuts and nice, fresh fruit.
At night he normally plays the flute.
I think he's neat and very cute,
My next-door neighbor, the little newt.

Oo

Odd Otter

In Ottawa there is an odd otter
Who floats on top of the water.
But on hot days she jogs
With the olive green frogs.
And she moves so fast,
  you won't spot her.

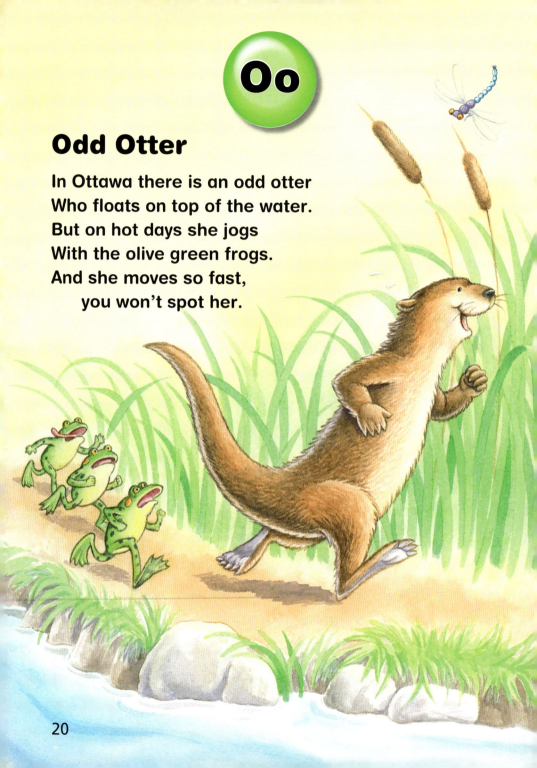

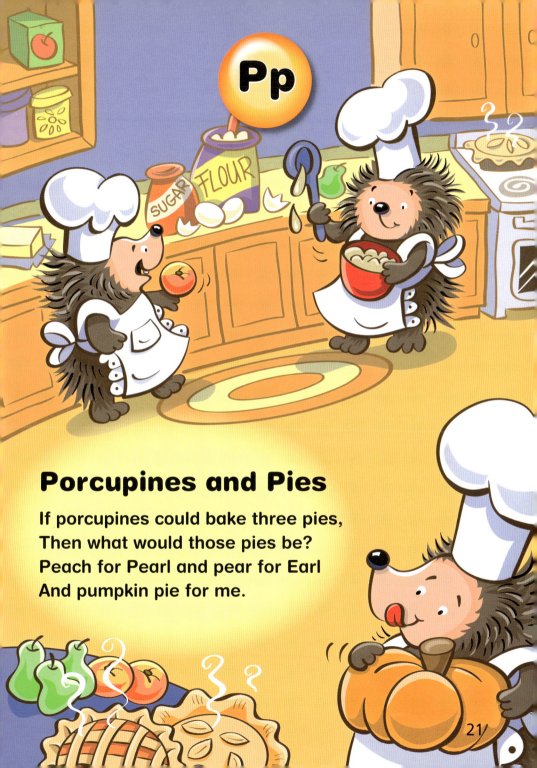

Porcupines and Pies

If porcupines could bake three pies,
Then what would those pies be?
Peach for Pearl and pear for Earl
And pumpkin pie for me.

21

Qq

Quiet Queen

The queen is quite quiet.
She quivers when she speaks.
If you ask her a question,
She quickly says, "Squeak, squeak."

22

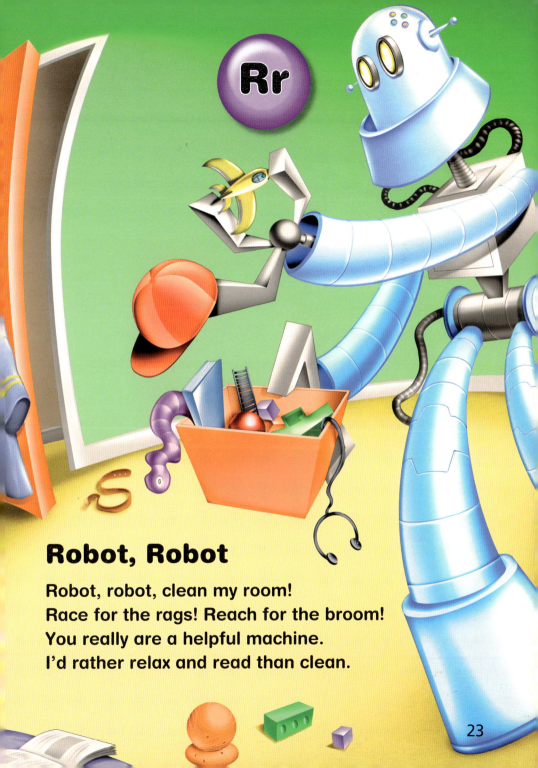

Robot, Robot

Robot, robot, clean my room!
Race for the rags! Reach for the broom!
You really are a helpful machine.
I'd rather relax and read than clean.

23

One Sunny Saturday

One sunny Saturday,
When I was feeling grand,
I sat by the sea and built a castle
Out of soft, wet sand.

My castle was so super,
Not such a little thing.
I put on a crown, went inside,
And pretended I was king.

Tiger's Tennis Lesson

Tiger takes tennis lessons
On Tuesdays, ten till noon.
Can you tell time, Tiger?
Better get to your lesson soon!

Under This Unusual Umbrella

Is it good luck
That I am stuck
Under this very unusual umbrella?
A duck and a pup
Are holding it up,
This very unusual umbrella!

Vv

Vultures on a Volcano

Vultures played violins on a volcano.
They were the bravest birds in town.
But every vulture vanished
When the lava came traveling down.

27

Wandering Wombat

Would a wombat wander
Across the Wild West?
Would he walk through windy weather
In a warm and woolly vest?

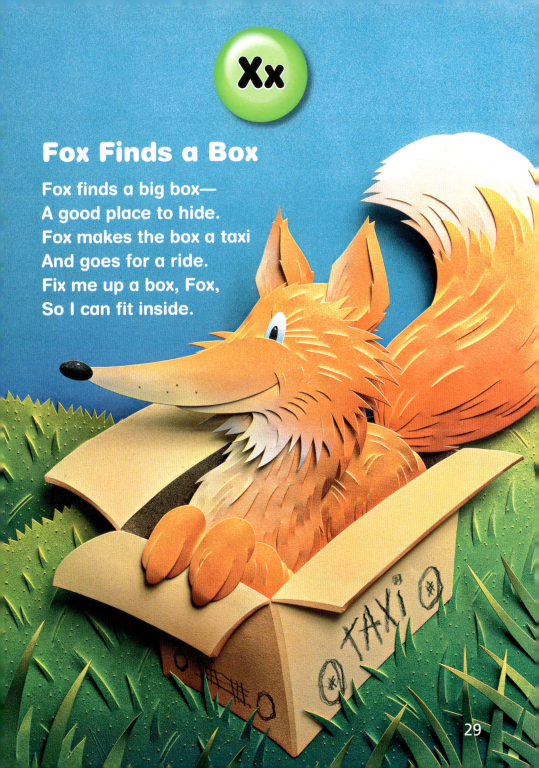

Fox Finds a Box

Fox finds a big box—
A good place to hide.
Fox makes the box a taxi
And goes for a ride.
Fix me up a box, Fox,
So I can fit inside.

A Yak in Our Yard

A yak came in our yard yesterday.
You can hear it loud and clear.
It's a young, yellow yak
With a yo-yo in its sack.
I'm afraid it may stay here all year.

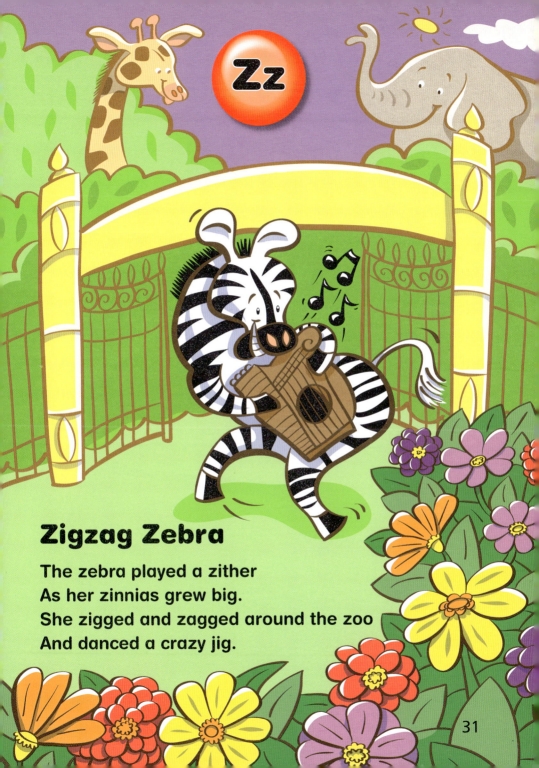

Zigzag Zebra

The zebra played a zither
As her zinnias grew big.
She zigged and zagged around the zoo
And danced a crazy jig.

31

The Last Rhyme

Our  ride has to end,
But you can always start again.
Hop on the bus anytime.
Pick a letter, read a rhyme.